The Persian Cat

A vet's guide on how to care for your persian cat

BY

DR. GORDON ROBERTS BVSC MRCVS

TABLE OF CONTENTS

INTRODUCTION

The Persian is an usual looking cat. They have a round head with large round eyes which can be blue, copper, green, hazel, or one of each. If you look at this cat in profile (side on), you will see the face is flat and the nose points upwards so you see the fleshy part of the nose. They have short but stocky body and thick legs with a thick neck which is also short, rather than the top as in other breeds. The average weight for a male Persian is 12lbs, whereas the female ranges from 8-12lbs. The Persian tail is short and they have relatively small ears for such a "large" cat. The coat on a Persian is thick, full and long, but each individual hair is fine, so they should look and feel lustrous and glossy.

Persians come in a number of colour variations but the most popular are solid colour, shaded and smoke, tabby and, tri and bi-colour. Calico is a unique tri-colour pattern. If the calico is mostly white this is known as a non-diluted calico with distinct patches of orange (or red) and black. In some cases, the black colour will be chocolate and if your cat has this colouring they are quite rare.

HISTORY

Persian cat origin theories tend to suggest the native land to be Iran, Turkey and Afghanistan. It is known that an Italy. A few years after that a Frenchman - Nicolas-Claude Fabri de Peiresc - was visitingItalian - Pietro della Valle, in the early 1600s, brought several long-haired cats from Persia, now known as Iran, to Angora ("Ankara") in Turkey and also brought back with him some long-haired cats

In the 1800s, England started breeding these Persian cats and so became known as the "second motherland to Persian Cats" even though the cats were then known as French cats. In England they were referred to as 'long-haired' rather than Persians and even now the British Cat Fanciers Club ruling is that each colouring is referred to as a separate cat breed.

Around the 1800s the long-haired cats were split into "Turkish Angora" and "Persian" and simply "long-haired". The Turkish Angora has a long flexible body, with a silky but less thick coat and large-pointed ears. The Persian on the other hand is considered a massive cat with a large round head and small ears, but was only referred to as Persian if it was blue in colour.

In the late 1800s in America, the Persian was known as a Persian in their Cat Clubs, unlike the UK, and all the long-haired cats were referred to as "the Persian cat".

CHARACTER

Persian cats have a gentle and sweet personality. With their long hair and cute flat faces they are a very attractive cat. Persians love people and don't require your constant attention unlike other breeds, the Siamese for example.

PERSIAN FACTS

- Named after Persia, country they originated.
- Most popular breed of Cat in the US.
- Teeth deteriorate at a much quicker rate because of flat face;

HEALTH

Persian cats are expected to live between 8 - 11 years. Pedigree cats are more likely to suffer from hereditory conditions, one for Persians is Polycystic Kidney Disease (PKD). PKD is an inherited kidney disease. Another that affects the heart is Hypertrophic Cardiomyopathy (HCM), and this too is inherited from an infected parent. Although the occurences are very low, Persians do inherit a tendency for developing cataracts. The flat face of a Persian means their teeth deteriorate at a much quick rate than other breeds. Keep an eye on their teeth and ensure they are kept clean.

Common Diseases

Polycystic Kidney Disease (PKD)

What is polycystic kidney disease?
Polycystic kidney disease (PKD) is an inherited condition in cats, that causes multiple cysts (pockets of fluid) to form in the kidneys. These cysts are present from birth.

They start out very small but they grow larger with time and may eventually severely disrupt the kidney; when that happens the kidney can no longer work and kidney failure develops. All cats that are affected by PKD have cysts in their kidneys, but the number of cysts present, and the rate at which the cysts grow is very variable. The cysts usually grow quite slowly, so most affected cats will not show any signs of kidney disease until relatively late in life, typically at around 7 or 8 years old, however in some cats kidney failure will occur at a much younger age while in other cats kidney failure will not develop until into old age. At the moment there is no way of predicting how rapidly the disease will progress in any particular cat.

Can PKD be cured?
Unfortunately there is no treatment that will prevent or delay the development of kidney failure in a cat that is affected by PKD. The cysts are present from birth and cannot be removed, nor can they be prevented from growing.

Once kidney failure has actually developed, treatment can be used to try to reduce the amount of work that the kidneys have to do, and to try to reverse the secondary effects of renal failure. Such treatment will improve the cat's quality of life, but will not alter the underlying disease or stop the cysts from growing larger.

It can be very difficult to identify PKD in its early stages when the cysts are very small. At this stage in the disease the kidneys will be working normally and the cat will show no outward signs of the disease. Even if your cat is regularly examined by your vet the kidneys will feel normal on palpation (feeling them through the body wall), they will look normal on an x-ray, and blood and urine tests will not show any abnormalities. Diagnosis at this early stage is most commonly achieved by examining the cat's kidneys using a high definition ultra-sound scanner to look for evidence of fluid filled cysts within the kidneys.

Recently a DNA test has also been developed that can identify affected cats. The test can be performed on either a blood sample or cheek swab. It has the advantage of being more accurate and does not need the expertise required for an ultrasound scan.

Once the cysts have grown large enough to disrupt kidney function signs of kidney failure will develop. Common signs of kidney failure include weight loss, poor appetite, increased thirst and increased urine production and occasionally vomiting. At this stage your vet may detect that the kidneys feel abnormal on palpation, and blood and urine tests will indicate that the kidneys are not working properly.

Even at this advanced stage an ultrasound scan is still the best way to confirm that the kidney failure is due to PKD rather than any other form of kidney disease.

How common is PKD in cats?

Unfortunately PKD has now become very common in some cat breeds. Persian cats have the highest incidence of problems and studies around the world and in the UK have shown that around 1 in 3 Persian cats are now affected by the disease. Other cat breeds that have been developed using Persian bloodlines, like Chinchillas and Exotics, also have a significant proportion of affected cats, but in other unrelated breeds it is a rare condition.

How is PKD inherited?

PKD is the result of a single, autosomal, dominant gene abnormality. This means that:

Every cat with the abnormal gene will have PKD, there are no unaffected carriers of the gene.

Every cat with PKD will have the abnormal gene and can pass the gene onto its kittens, even if that cat only has a few small cysts in its kidneys.

A cat only needs one of its parents to be affected with PKD in order to inherit the abnormal gene and be affected itself.

Every breeding cat with PKD will pass the disease on to a proportion of its kittens, even if it is mated with an unaffected cat.

What can be done about PKD?

PKD has become very common in some breeds of cat because it doesn't usually cause kidney failure until quite late in life, so an affected cat may have been used to produce a large number of litters of kittens before it becomes ill itself. Many cat breeders are now aware of this problem, and are trying to identify affected cats at a young age, before they have been used for breeding.

The Feline Advisory Bureau (FAB) has now set up a nationwide screening program to identify which cats are affected and to allow breeders to make informed decisions about which cats to use for future breeding. The FAB screening program involves either an ultrasound examination of the cats kidneys by one of a panel of approved, highly qualified veterinary ultrasonographers, or a DNA test. A FAB approved certificate stating the result of the scan or DNA test for that particular cat is then issued.

Anyone who is planning to buy a Persian cat or kitten should make sure that the cat, or both of its parents, have been checked by an experienced ultrasonographer using a high quality ultrasound machine, or had the DNA test before they buy the cat.

Urinary Tract Stones

What is cystitis?

Cystitis is a general term referring to inflammation in the urinary bladder. The term cystitis does not imply a specific underlying cause.

In cats, diseases of the lower urinary tract (the bladder and urethra) are grouped under the term 'feline lower urinary tract disease' (FLUTD) as it can be difficult sometimes to distinguish between diseases of the bladder and urethra (the exit to the bladder), as many diseases will affect both structures.

What are the signs of FLUTD?

Typical signs in cats with FLUTD are those of inflammation and irritation of the lower urinary tract. The common signs are therefore:
- Increased frequency and urgency of urination.
- Difficulty in urinating (spending a long time straining on the litter tray while passing only small quantities of urine).
- The presence of blood in the urine.

Occasionally complete obstruction to the passage of urine (straining persistently without producing any urine).

With the latter sign particularly (straining without the passage of any urine), it is important to seek urgent veterinary attention as complete blockage to the flow of urine can be a life-threatening complication if left untreated.

What causes FLUTD?

There are a vast number of potential causes of FLUTD, but in many cats there may be severe inflammation of the bladder and/or ure-thra without an identifiable underlying cause (so called 'idiopathic' FLUTD). These idiopathic cases have to be differentiated from other potential causes of the clinical signs though so that appropriate treatment can be given. Some of the potential causes of FLUTD are listed below:

- Idiopathic (inflammation for no known cause)
- Urinary calculi ('bladder stones') Bacterial infections
- Neoplasia (tumour) Anatomical abnormalities
- Urethral plugs (blockage of urethra with a mixture of crystals or small calculi/stones and inflammatory material)

The initial diagnosis of FLUTD is based on the identification of signs of lower urinary tract inflammation. The clinical signs displayed by the cat are often characteristic of FLUTD, but may have to be differentiated from straining to pass faeces (constipation). Furthermore the signs displayed do not help to differentiate the cause of FLUTD.

Initially, a cat with uncomplicated FLUTD may not require any treatment. However, if the signs continue, or if there is recurrence of the clinical signs further investigation may be required to identify the underlying cause of the FLUTD.

What further investigations are required to diagnose FLUTD?

Where clinical signs are persistent or recurrent, a number of investigations may be required to differentiate idiopathic FLUTD from the other known causes of urinary tract inflammation. These investigations may include:

- Laboratory analysis of a urine sample
- Bacterial culture of a urine sample Blood samples to look for other evidence of urinary tract disease or other systemic disease Radiographs (x-rays) of the bladder and urethra (performed under a general anaesthetic)
- Ultrasound examination of the bladder

The information from these investigations should help to identify a specific underlying cause if one is present. If these tests do not identify a specific cause then the FLUTD is classified as idiopathic.

What is the treatment for FLUTD?

The most important treatment for most cases of FLUTD is to increase the cats water intake. The easiest way of doing thisis to feed a tinned food, rather than a dry food, and more water can also be added to the food. Some cats also need to be encouraged to drink more water and your veterinary surgeon can give you further tips as to how this may be achieved. Further treatment depends on the underlying cause.

For example:

Cases of idiopathic disease may respond to treatment with anti-inflammatory or analgesic (pain-relieving) drugs, but it is crucial that you only use drugs specifically prescribed by your veterinary surgeon, as may human products are extremely dangerous to use in cats. For cats with persistent or recurring clinical signs a variety of other drugs may also be tried.

Bacterial infections of the lower urinary tract, although uncommon in cats, will usually respond well to antibiotic therapy.

If a cat develops a blocked urethra (this almost exclusively occurs in males), emergency treatment is required to remove the blockage, which may require flushing of the urethra while the cat is given a short anaesthetic.

If bladder stones (calculi) are present they may have to be removed surgically or, depending on their type, they may be able to be dissolved by using a special diet, or dietary additive.

There is no universal treatment for FLUTD. Each case has to be investigated to determine the underlying cause, and then the treatment has to be tailored to the individual cat. Sometimes despite appropriate investigation and treatment clinical signs may still recur.

How can FLUTD be prevented?

It is impossible to completely prevent diseases of the lower urinary tract occurring. However, FLUTD is more common in cats that have a lower water consumption, cats from a multi-cat household, and in cats that are inactive and obese. All these factors may relate, at least in part, to the frequency with which a cat urinates. Avoidance of obesity and encouraging exercise may be of some help in preventing FLUTD, and as cats tend to drink very little the feeding of at least some tinned food rather than exclusively a dry cat food product will help to maintain a higher water intake.

If a cat develops urinary calculi (stones), the feeding of special diets (available from veterinary surgeons) may help to prevent recurrence of stone formation. In most other situations there is probably little necessity to alter the cat's diet

Mammary Tumours

What is this tumour?

This is a tumour originating from cells of the mammary glands. Most tumours are potentially or already malignant so early surgical removal is important to prevent spread to other parts of the body (metastasis). A cat may have multiple tumours, sometimes of different types, within different mammary glands.

What do we know about the cause?

The reason why a particular pet may develop this, or any cancer, is not straightforward. Cancer is often seemingly the culmination of a series of circumstances which come together for the unfortunate individual. Cancer is non-lethal genetic damage of cells (mutations in the DNA genome). Some cats have a genetic tendency to develop cancer and the risk increases with increasing age. However, sex hormones are the most important single factor increasing the risk of a cat developing mammary tumours.

If the ovaries and uterus are removed by ovariohysterectomy (spaying) at an early age, there will be less risk of these tumours developing. Conversely, giving a cat female sex hormones increases the incidence.

Cancer induction is a multistep process and the early, pre-cancerous stages are hyperplasias and dysplasia (overgrowth and abnormal growth). These stages are under hormonal disturbances. They continue to be influenced by hormones and are not freely proliferating (growing) entities without function. In cats, most such precancerous changes can progress to true cancers.

In some species of animal, viruses are important factors in inducing mammary cancer. Viruses have been found within these tumours in cats but, as far as we are aware, they do not cause the tumours.

Why has my animal developed this cancer?

Some animals have a greater tendency (genetic susceptibility) to cancer. The more divisions a cell undergoes, the more probable is a mutation so cancer is commoner in older animals. Mammary tumours begin their abnormal growth under the influence of hormones but if they progress to a malignant stage removing hormones does not affect the course of the tumour

Are these common tumours?

These are common tumours in female cats, mainly in middleaged to older animals. Pre-cancerous hyperplasias and dysplasias account for 22% of mammary lumps, benign cancers for 0.9% and malignant cancers for 77%. The Siamese breed is three times more likely to develop mammary tumours than Domestic Shorthaired cats. Persian cats also develop tumours frequently.

Mammary tumours in cats are commoner in Scandinavian countries because spaying of domestic cats is not commonly practised and the female hormone progesterone is sometimes used to prevent pregnancy.

Although most cats with these tumours are elderly, malignant tumours can occur in cats as young as two years of age. Mammary tumours are rare in male cats, but do occur.

How will this cancer affect my pet?

The most obvious effect is a lump or multiple lumps in the mammary glands. Some tumours produce secretion (clear, milky or blood-stained fluid which may be expressed from a teat). Benign tumours rarely ulcerate or bleed but ulceration of malignant tumours is not uncommon. Malignant tumours are often firmly attached to the surrounding structures with poorly demarcated edges.

Large tumours may lose some of their blood supply so parts of them degenerate. They may have physical effects by pressing into the surrounding tissues. Inflammation and secondary infection are possible with pain and general signs of illness.

If the cancer spreads (metastasises) to the lungs, there may be shortness of breath and difficulty breathing. Weight loss due to loss of body fat and muscle may occur in the later stages of malignant cancer.

 The immune system is often damaged, which allows   cancers to develop and infections to persist.

How is this cancer diagnosed?
Clinically, these tumours are diagnosed by the typical appearance. Accurate diagnosis of the type (and therefore how it will behave) relies upon microscopic examination of tissue.

Cytology, the microscopic examination of cell samples, is not an accurate method of diagnosis for this group of tumours.

Accurate diagnosis, prediction of behaviour (prognosis) and a microscopic assessment of whether the tumour has been fully removed rely on microscopic examination of tissue (histopathology).

This is done at a specialised laboratory by a veterinary pathologist. The piece of tissue examined always needs to include the edges of the lump. Examination of the whole lump will indicate whether the cancer has been fully removed.

The histopathology report typically includes words that indicate whether a tumour is 'benign' (non-spreading, local growth) or 'malignant' (capable of spreading to other body sites). These, together with the origin or type of tumour, the grade (degree of resemblance to normal cells or 'differentiation') and stage (how large it is and extent of spread) indicate how the cancer is likely to behave.

What types of treatment are available?

The commonest treatment is surgical removal of the lump. Sometimes this is just the lump and sometimes the whole gland and draining lymph node are removed. Many glands and lymph nodes may be removed if there are several tumours.

Spaying (ovariohysterectomy) early in life reduces the incidence of cancer. Spaying at the time of tumour removal does not affect growths that are already cancerous but can cause .some precancerous hyperplasias to regress and disappear. It is unlikely to help reduce further tumour development.

Early mammary tumours are hormone dependent but the hormones involved are different in different species. Medical treatments used in women are unsuitable for use in cats.

Can this cancer disappear without treatment?

Spaying does not affect established cancer or prevent recurrence. Development of cancer is a multi-step process so it may stop at some stages but all these cancers have the potential to progress to malignancy, usually rapidly within months. As they have this potential, early surgical removal is always recommended. Very occasionally, spontaneous loss of blood supply to the cancer can make it die but the dead tissue will still need surgical removal. The body's immune system is not effective in causing these tumours to regress.

How can I nurse my pet?

Preventing your pet from rubbing, scratching, licking or biting the tumour will reduce itching, inflammation, ulceration, infection and bleeding. Any ulcerated area needs to be kept clean. After surgery, the operation site similarly needs to be kept clean and your pet should not be allowed to interfere with the site. Any loss of sutures or significant swelling or bleeding should be reported to your veterinary surgeon. If you require additional advice on post-surgical care, please ask.

Histopathology will give your veterinary surgeon the diagnosis that will indicate the type and how it is likely to behave. There is significant variation between animals in their response to tumours and the probability of further tumour development.

Any mammary lesion may be inflamed (mastitis) and a few lumps are solely due to inflammation.

Benign non-cancerous growths are hyperplasias (overgrowth) and dysplasias (abnormal growth). They include those arising from the epithelium that normally produces milk (lobular or epithelial hyperplasia, occasionally called 'adenosis'), growth including the connective tissue between the glands as well (fibroadenomatous change or fibroepithelial hyperplasia) and growth due to expansion of the ducts that take the milk to the teats (cystic ducts, ductal ectasia or hyperplasia).

Benign cancers are adenomas. Some arise only from the milk-producing epithelium (simple adenomas). Others include other tissues such as the myoepithelium and connective tissue between the glands and are a progression of fibroadenomatous change.

Malignant cancerous growths develop from the epithelium that normally produces milk or the ducts (simple carcinoma or adenocarcinoma). As well as the type of tumour, the clinical stage it has reached and the mitotic index (number of cells dividing) and whether there is local invasion are important factors in behaviour.

When will I know if the cancer is permanently cured?

'Cure' has to be a guarded term in dealing with any cancer. It is very difficult to promise complete cure once your cat has developed mammary tumours but the following general guidelines may help. In cats, most hyperplasias progress to neoplasia.

Mammary tumours are age dependent so an older queen will have a higher probability of recurrence and the proportion of malignant tumours increases with age.

Tumours of less than 2 cm diameter at the time of surgery have a median postoperative survival of 3 years. Tumours greater than 3 cm diameter have a median survival of less than six months. Most secondary tumours are in lungs and, in contrast to women, rarely in bones.

Multiple tumours are also common. Growth in the different glands is usually multifocal in origin and not spread from a single initial site. It is therefore advisable to have your cat checked frequently to ensure there is no regrowth of a tumour and no new ones have appeared.

Are there any risks to my family or other pets?
No, these are not infectious tumours and are not transmitted from pet to pet or from pets to people.

PROTECTING YOUR CAT FROM PARASITES

stages of their lives. Kittens are likely to be infected with worms even before birth! The good news is that there are plenty of things you can do to deal with the problem.

Fleas

Fleas are nasty little parasites. An infestation can be unpleasant and possibly even dangerous for your cat, yourself and your family. Fleas feed on your cats' blood and in serious cases they can even make your cat anaemic. This can cause your cat to become extremely unwell… possibly even critically ill. They cause severe itching, which may lead to fur loss and sores from continual scratching. Their bites are equally uncomfortable for humans, causing intense itching, redness and inflammation

To be able to treat fleas effectively, it is good idea to understand how their life cycle works. This comprises three stages…

Stage 1

The adult flea jumps onto your pet and begins feeding on their blood. This is when irritation begins and your pet begins scratching non-stop.

Stage 2

In under 48 hours, the fleas will begin to lay their eggs, which will fall off your pet into their surroundings (i.e. your home!). A female flea can lay up to 50 eggs per day & 10 females can lay up to 15,000 eggs!

Stage 3

Within days all these eggs will hatch into flea larvae. Because the larvae don't like light they crawl into dark areas (such as carpets, cracks and crevices) around your home. The larvae then turn into adult fleas and Stage 1 begins anew…

Statistics show that only 5% of fleas in your home will actually be living on your pet – the other 95% (eggs and larvae) will actually be living in your carpets and furniture. It's therefore essential that the problem is dealt with before it gets out of control. When your pet has fleas, you may see black specs throughout their coat (these are flea droppings) or they may be scratching more than normal, possibly to the extent that they start losing fur.

You should immediately seek advice from your vet on what flea products are right for your pet and the environment they live in to prevent the problem escalating.

There are many flea products available, but please be aware some only kill the adult fleas on your pet at the time of using the treatment and won't kill adults around the home, which will be able to just jump back on.

Worms

Worms are an internal parasite that will affect your cat throughout their entire life if left unchecked. Worms can cause many undesirable side effects to your pet's health such as diarrhea, vomiting, swollen abdomen, discomfort and respiratory problems. In some cases, worms carried by our pets can cause some very serious side-effects in adults and children. Fortunately, regular worming treatment for all of your pets can prevent this.

Some common types of worms are:

Roundworms

Roundworms are the most common internal parasite in cats. Kittens are even likely to be infected at birth, because roundworm larvae can be directly passed onto the young via their mother's milk. Other ways your pet may become infected with round that may have eaten roundworm eggs. The roundworm can also be passed between animals by contact with infected feces. Roundworm infections can be passed to humans and if left untreated can cause serious health problems (including blindness). If children play in areas such as sand or dirt piles that contain infected feces they may pick up worm larvae on their hands.

If their hands aren't washed properly, the child could ingest the larvae when eating or sucking their thumb and end up with roundworms.

Tapeworms

Your cat may become infected with tapeworm when they groom themselves. This is because they may eat fleas or lice in their fur which have previously fed on a tapeworm. They can also become infected by eating infected rodents

The tapeworm lives in the small intestine and steals lots of the nutrients from the food your cat eats. You may even see the tapeworm, which looks like a rice grain, under your pet's tail, or in their feces.

The best treatment for tapeworm is to make sure your cat is free from fleas and regularly de-wormed.

It is always best to prevent worms rather than only treating the problem once your cat is already suffering the effects of worm infestation. So contact your vet early on to find the best worm treatment protocol for your cat. Pregnant or young cats will require different treatments to adult cats, so please seek your vet's advice if you are unsure.

THE IMPORTANCE OF VACCINATION

We've already established that it's better to prevent illness than to cure it, so it's really important to make sure that your pet is protected by vaccination from the most common diseases. Vaccines have considerably reduced the number of pets that die from fatal diseases each year, so there's simply no reason not to make sure your pet is fully protected.

Bear in mind that any cat traveling abroad requires a rabies vaccination by law. Kittens should be vaccinated at around 9 weeks and then again at 12 weeks of age. The kitten will need both vaccines to stimulate their immune system. After this, it is recommended that your adult cat has a yearly booster vaccination to keep the level of immunity constant.

The Truth About Neutering

The decision to neuter your cat is never easy – something not helped by the many 'old wives tales' on this subject (none of which are actually supported by medical research). It goes without saying that neutering prevents unwanted pregnancies, but it actually has purposes beyond that. For any pet, neutering presents both advantages and disadvantages, so do some research before making your decision...

Should I have my cat neutered?

Queens

There is no medical reason for letting your cat have a litter beforen neutering, so neuter them early. Queens can be neutered any time between 4-6 months old.

Neutering lowers the risk of your cat catching deadly viruses, such as FIV and FELV (feline AIDS and leukemia), from tom cats who have not been health screened. These could be passed from the mother to her kitten.

When a queen reaches sexual maturity she will 'call' for a mate for approximately one week out of every 2-3 until she has found one. If you are not breeding from the queen, this calling is extremely noisy and will likely prove irritating to both you and your neighbors. In addition, the queen can become grumpy and irritable if not mated, so neutering can keep her in a good mood! Neutering eliminates the risk of uterine infections and lowers the risk of breast cancer.

Toms

Neutering will help to prevent a lot of undesirable behaviour, such as spraying urine to 'mark his territory'. This is a very strong odour and can be difficult to remove from the areas sprayed, so it's better to circumvent it altogether. As with queens, toms can be neutered anytime between 4-6 months old.

An un-castrated tom will want to mark his territory outside as well. This can cause him to stray long distances, potentially getting lost or injured.

He is also more likely to fight to try and show his dominance to other male cats. Wounds sustained in fights can result in severe infection and abscesses and will almost certainly require a vet's attention. Statistics show that un-castrated males have a much higher chance of contracting the incurable diseases.

FOOD AND DIET

Cats are inherently possessive about the food they eat, and the water they drink. Their ancestors had to fight off others whenever they wanted a meal, and even current day wild or feral relatives of domestic cats don't know where their next meal will come from. Your cat has food available every day, of course, but these habits are deeply ingrained.

Drinking Behavior

It is vital for a cat, like any animal, to drink healthy amounts of water each day.

Water doesn't seem like a nutrient, but it does account for two-thirds of your cat's body weight. It is the basis for all of the chemical processes in her body.

Water transports all your cat's necessary oxygen and nutrients through her body. Water carries these essentials through the cat's bloodstream and into her cells. It moisturizes air located in her lungs and regulates her body temperature. Water is also essential in the elimination of waste products after your cat metabolizes everything she needs from her food and drink.

Cats Fed Wet Food Don't Need a Lot of Water

Your cat's water requirements are based almost totally on her food's moisture content. Wild cats get most of the water they need from prey that has been freshly killed. Your cat can go for a long time without water, as long as her canned food contains a high moisture percentage. If the moisture level in her food drops below 61%, she will need extra water. You probably already have a water bowl for her, right beside her food bowl.

Even your domestic cat has a thirst drive, and she will guard her food, since that is where she is accustomed to getting the fluid she needs. Her ancestors and wild relatives will fight to the death to defend their prey. Even if she is dehydrated, though, your domestic cat will not initiate drinking as dogs do.

Guarding Food

Cats may do well on dry foods, but canned foods are healthier in many ways for her. Your cat probably wouldn't care as much if your dog sneaks in and steals some of her dry food, but she will react much more violently if the dog tries to take her canned food.

Your domestic cat may even react to your dog's attempt to make off with her dry food. It is so ingrained in her psyche to guard her food that she may protect even food she is not intent on eating in the next few days.

A cat's urinary tract is much healthier if it has the appropriate amount of fluid within it. Cats are all carnivores, despite what some cat food manufacturers might tell you. They count on their meat to get the fluids their body needs.

Cats are inherently able to get most of their water requirements through their kill. Therefore, it is most understandable then, that your domestic cat protects her food so fiercely. It is hard wired into her psyche the protein your cat gets from animal tissue is different from plant protein, which her body is not well adapted to use properly. Dogs and humans are adapted to take in plant proteins.

Cats are not. One of their most essential nutrients is taurine. It is found in meat but not in plants. Lack of this nutrient can cause heart problems and blindness for cats.

Why You Should Cut Down On Treats

There can be a number of reasons why you're cat may be over-weight. However, the most likely cause is an unsuitable diet.

Food plays an important role on your cat's overall health and well-being. A nutritious, balanced and healthy diet is an essential part of an active lifestyle, and a big part of that is resisting the temptation to give them human food as treats.

Although it may seem harmless, if your cat begins to expect occasional treats like this, it can have a serious effect on their overall health. Just look at these comparisons…

5kg Cat	Average Human
25g cheese	3.5 hamburgers
1 glass of milk	6.5 large muffins
1 crisp	0.5 chocolate bar

As you can see, these foods can be extremely unhealthy for your pets, even in small amounts. It's therefore essential that you resist the temptation to offer them treats like this (no matter how much they beg!). There are plenty of healthy pet treats available which pets love, so keep a supply of those around the house instead.

Signs that your pet is overweight include…
- You can't easily feel the ribs when running your hands along your their sides
- There is no obvious slimming at your pet's waist
- Their collar or harness may become tight and need loosening
- They may not exercise as much and become tired quickly
- Slow, lethargic movement
- Shortness of breath
- Stiffness in joints
- Sleeping more than normal
- Bad temper

If you feel you're cat may be showing any of the signs above contact your vet. They will be able to offer advice on weight loss and healthy eating for your pet. When planning a diet for your cat, pick a high-quality food that's rich in protein. There are many foods available but, some will be more suited to your cat than others, so don't be afraid to ask your vet for advice if you're unsure.

LEARN TO SPOT EARLY WARNING SIGNS

You know your cat best and if you notice any abnormal symptoms or changes in behaviour, do not hesitate to visit your vet for advice or reassurance. Vets love to talk with you about your animals, and will always be pleased to give their professional advice!

Even if it turns out to be something completely innocuous, you'll still have the peace of mind that comes from knowing they're in good health.

Some signs to look out for include:
- Change in weight (loss or gain)
- Changes in appetite
- Increased thirst
- Lethargy
- Stiffness/reluctance to exercise as normal
- Change in their coat
- Changes in urination patterns (including incontinence)
- Coughing and wheezing
- Breathlessness
- Vomiting, diarrhea or constipation
- Smelly breath
- Eyesight or hearing problem

It is important to make sure your cat has twice-yearly check-ups with their vet. This will help to make sure any illnesses or health problems they may be suffering from are detected in the earliest stages.

Keeping Your Persian's Teeth Healthy

Dental disease is the number one health disorder found in cats over 3 years of age, with more than 70% of cats suffering from some form of dental disease.

Dental disease has been referred to as a 'silent killer' of our pets, because the bacteria on your cat's teeth can move into the blood stream where it is free to travel to the heart, liver, lungs and kidneys. This will have a serious effect on your cat's overall health and may even compromise their immune system.

 Maintaining the health of your cat's teeth is therefore one of the most important things you can do to increase the comfort and length of their life.

People often mistakenly think that because their cats are eating, their teeth are fine. However, this is not necessarily the case. A cat's survival instinct is very strong, so it will continue to eat even with extremely sore and rotten teeth.

Our cats usually start life with shiny white teeth and healthy pink gums. Over time, the accumulation of plaque (bacteria) on the surface of the teeth will lead to inflammation of the gums (gingivitis). This will then lead to an accumulation of tartar (bacteria and minerals) on the surface of the teeth (and very bad breath!). If left untreated, bacteria will penetrate below the gum-line and can destroy supportive structures (periodontitis), leading to tooth-loss and abscesses.

Just think of any bad experiences you've had with toothache… Untreated dental conditions are often just as painful for pets as for people, so it's essential they are dealt with… and even better if they are prevented from occurring in the first place.

The good news is that dental disease is preventable if treated early enough, so have your vet regularly check your pet's teeth for any early warning signs.

Treatment at the vets involves a light anesthetic and possible dental x-rays. These will give the vet a clear picture of the health of the tooth roots and the jaw, as these crucial areas are not visible to the naked eye.

The vet will clean all the teeth with an ultrasonic dental machine, which cleans away the bacteria beneath the gum line. Afterwards, the vet will assess each tooth individually and decide if further treatment is required. If the dental disease has progressed too far on some of the teeth, the vet will recommend a tooth extraction. It may sound drastic, but it will solve the problem once and for all and leave your pet much more comfortable in the future. There's also plenty you can do at home to take care of your pet's teeth.

It is best to start dental home care when your pet is young. This is one of the most important things to do to help prevent dental disease. Introduce regular tooth brushing while your pet is still young, so they become used to it. This will help to prevent the build up of plaque. However, some dental diseases are genetic, so home care can cure the symptoms, but never get rid of the disease completely.

A wide range of home care products are available, including chews, toys and mouth washes. However, it has been proven that brushing is the number one preventative measure owners can take. As always, ask your vet if you need advice about which products are right for your pet.

LEARN TO SPOT EARLY WARNING SIGNS

Persian cats need grooming at least every day, sometimes you may find the need to do a quick groom in between! Their thick long coats will matt if not combed on a regular basis and if matts are allowed to form they will cause your cat severe discomfort and will in extreme cases need to be cut off.

You will notice in the winter that your cat's coat will thicken up quite considerably so more grooming will be required. Grooming will also help to prevent the dreaded hairballs.

If you would prefer not to groom on a daily basis, some owners opt for a short coat and the style is referred to as a lion cut, with the head, legs and some of the tail left unshaven, whilst the body fur is shaved fairly short.

If you have a Persian with a light coloured face you will notice tear staining. Keeping tear staining at bay is a challenge, daily or even hourly wiping won't necessarily remove the staining.

As well as brushing and combing, you should also check your cats nails and their ears for foreign bodies. Indoor cats won't wear their nails out as much as outdoor cats and nails shouldn't be allowed to become too long. Clipping them will also help to prevent your furniture being scratched.

Static fur can sometimes be a problem, if your cat suffers from this try the following:

- use metal combs and brushes - avoid plastic ones;
- lay a wet paper towel on the fur during grooming;
- buy an anti-static spray from reputable pet store;
- before touching your cat's fur, rub some handcream into your hands

EXERCISE

Persians are not noted for their energy, so it is essential adequate exercise to stay fit and healthy.

Although Persians are more than happy to play with you, play with interactive toys, that you play with your Persian to ensure they get the chase balls etc., you will need to keep reminding and encouraging them to do, it isn't something they will do automatically on a regular basis! However, having said that they do exhibit sudden bursts of lively activity - quite kitten-like - running around the room and rolling about.

TRAINING

Cats are independent creatures and will only respond to training by using a quite calm voice and lots of stroking. Persian kittens are no different to any other cat and require the same patience as any other pet

Cats have their own ways of marking territory, and even their people. Your cat may have rubbed her face along the side of your hand, and if she does this with her mouth involved, she may be marking you as her own person.

It's not like a slobbery dog kiss, but she is letting you know that you are hers, and cat fans find this appealing in its own way.

You'll never know everything your cat is thinking, since she is a creature unlike any other. Cats will never be an open book for humans, but perhaps that is one of the reasons we find cats so interesting.

Vocalizations

 Cats have a unique type of vocalization used to communicate with other cats and with their people, as well. When you share your home with a cat or cats, you should become familiar with the sounds and nuances of your individual cats' vocabularies.
When your cat speaks to you, you need to know whether she is fearful, playful or simply hungry. Once you learn her language, you can share more of your cat's life and be a bigger part of that life.

Domestic cats are believed to develop more sophisticated language patterns as compared to feral and wild cats. Perhaps that is because some of their language is used to converse with us.

Meow

This is the sound most often associated with cats, but some cats never make this exact sound. Whatever the variation, your cat usually uses a meow as a greeting, either to you or to other cats.

Mew

Kittens mew when they want attention from their mothers. A mew will become louder if your cat is fearful, or in distress. Some cats mew instead of making the more typical "meow" that people use to describe general cat language.

Chirp

Chirps are high-pitched, short sounds that cats often use to express their anticipation of receiving something they enjoy. This may mean a treat, affection, or playtime. Chirps are sometimes used to get attention.

Purring

The purr is a motor-like, vibrating sound that humans associate with contentment. Actually, it may also be used by a cat to comfort herself if she is in pain or experiencing anxiety. Veterinarians have noticed cats purring when they are in pain, so it is believed that cats use the purring to soothe themselves. Mother cats typically purr to their kittens to give them security and comfort. The subtle or strong vibrations are also helpful for kittens to use to find their mother in her nest. Newborn kittens cannot hear or see, so they can feel mother near through vibration.

Growl

There is no mistaking a growl when you hear one. It is usually a simple warning before a cat gets violent. It may also be used to scare off a perceived foe before it comes to violence. Some cats become possessive of their food, and may growl at an interloper who might want to steal some of it.

Hiss

This sound brings to mind those made by snakes. It usually only lasts several seconds. It is a warning to others to stay away. It may be loud or quiet, depending on the cat and the circumstances. Hissing can help a cat who is low in the pecking order become more respected if it is believed to be serious by her cat compatriots.

Spit

A spit is a very short sound that sounds like popping. It is especially vocal if the entrance of another cat startles your kitty. Spitting may be heard before or after hissing, and often times the spit will be used just before a cat runs away. This is especially true with cats that are naturally timid.

Squeak

This sound is high-pitched and raspy, and is usually made when your cat anticipates that something good is coming. Treats or meals may elicit squeaks. Sometimes cats also squeak when they are playing.

Shriek

This is a high-pitched, harsh sound that is used in aggression or in painful situations. You are most likely to hear a cat shriek when she is fighting another cat. It can be a scary sound, especially since is not typically heard that often.

Chirrup

This is also called a trill. It is a sound that incorporates purring and meowing. It is usually a very happy sound and is sometimes used as a greeting.

Caterwaul

This is an awful sound and is made by mating cats. You may hear it late at night close to your home. Spayed and neutered cats make better pets and you won't have to listen to this sound, at least in your home, if your cats are fixed.

Murmur

Murmuring sounds a bit like a trill or chirrup. It is a quiet, soft sound that is made with your cat's mouth closed. Mother cats murmur to their young. It may be used as part of a greeting ritual by your cat when you come home from work. In this case, purring and rubbing often follow it.

Chatter

This is an "ack-ack" type of sound that is softly uttered when your cat sees a bird or squirrel outside a window. There may be almost no sound actually heard. Humans believe the chatter means that their cat is frustrated, but only the cats know for sure.

Moan

Moaning is low, mournful and sad, and is sometimes heard just before your cat coughs or vomits. Elderly cats may make the sound if they are lost. When used in the presence of people, it usually means that your cat needs your help, or at least your reassurance.

This is one of the most intriguing of vocalizations, but it technically may not be a vocalization at all. The motion for meowing is made with the mouth, but there is no sound. Some people believe that this sound may be of a pitch that is too high for humans to hear. Silent meows are wonderful, even though they are noiseless.

Vocal Variations among Cats

These vocalizations are generalized and not all cats sound the same when they make the same titled noise. Some sounds have more than one meaning, depending on the situation and cat involved. You probably hear your cat talk during the day and know exactly what she means.

Kitten mews are among the friendliest of cat sounds, generally of a higher tone than some of the more unpleasant sounds they may make later in life. The vocal pattern and tone of sounds made by cats indicate whether the cat is feeling friendly or decidedly unfriendly.

Friendly cat sounds are usually higher on the tonal scale and they move from high notes to low. Sounds made with friendly intent are usually shorter in duration than angry or fretful sounds. Sounds made by urgent cats move from lower to higher ranges. The sound may increase in volume if your cat is angry or upset.

Cats who have outgoing and friendly dispositions are often quite vocal with their chosen people. Your cat may string together various friendly sounds, as though she is forming sentences to speak with you. She probably expects that you will talk back.

Some cats may be perfectly friendly and happy, but simply not as vocal. These cats are more likely to use body language to let you know what they want. You can almost converse without words, once a non-vocal cat lets you know her signs. Just because your cat doesn't talk doesn't mean she doesn't want you to speak to her. She probably will enjoy your voice even if she is not talkative herself.

Even cats in the same family will commonly develop different vocalizations and vocabularies. You may have two sisters from the same litter, and one may be quite vocal, while the other makes more use of body language than voice. Some cats greet you with a "hello" meow when they enter the room, and some won't. Those that don't speak will usually rub on you or otherwise communicate with you.

Your cat may be more likely to speak with you if you speak to her often. It's not a guarantee, but she may feel more like speaking if you are an active participant in the conversations.

Cats get a feeling of security from hearing your voice. The tone and cadence you use with your cat can mimic that of mothers talking to human babies. The rhythm and tone is the same, and is nurturing and calming to hear. Since cats are small and dependent on you for their care, speaking to them with a calm and supportive voice is natural, and it is healthy for your cats.

Body Language

Even if her vocalizations do not fully tell you how your cat is feeling about something or someone, her body language will. Cats use many signals, including facial expressions and body posturing, which convey their message and help them in avoiding confrontations. When you learn about feline posture, you can deepen your bond with your cat and prevent the misunderstanding of her expressions.

The "Halloween" Cat Pose

You've probably seen cardboard and plastic cats made for the witching season. The cat has her back arched and looks very defensive. Your cat's tail tells you a lot about her mood. When she holds her tail high, it means that she is confident. If it curls around your leg, it signals her friendliness towards you. When it is tucked between or below the legs, it means that your cat is anxious or insecure.

The full-fur, upright tail means your cat feels threatened. If you combine that with an arched back and hair that is upright along her spine, this means "Back off". Your cat probably never uses this position with you, but she may with unfamiliar cats or other animals or people.

The Relaxed Cat

Your cat, when relaxed, has ears at rest or pointed slightly forward and to the side. This position indicates that she is content and feels neither aggressive nor fearful. She may even roll over on her back when you pet her, and this means she is quite relaxed. In other circumstances, the roll-over may mean other things. However, if she is quite comfortable with you, she may be looking for a tummy rub.

Cat Eyes

Many cats find direct stares to be threatening, depending on the situation. In a social setting, your cat may seek out a person who is ignoring her. She perceives this inattention as a non-threatening gesture.

When your cat becomes fearful, her pupils expand. This allows them to take in the most information, visually, about a situation. If your cat's eyes have pupils fully dilated, she is probably quite frightened, and may wish to retreat.

In angry or aroused cats, the pupil often narrows or constricts, which helps cats to focus on important details. Your cat's eyes also respond to indoor or outdoor lighting, so narrow pupils may simply mean that there is a good deal of light in the area.

Cat Ear Movements

If your cat is nervous or agitated, her ears are probably twitching. She may be looking for reassurance if she is nervous, so offer it to her. Medical issues may also lead to persistent ear twitching, so take your cat to the vet if you suspect this might be the problem.

When your cat is interested and alert, or if something captures her attention, her ears will usually be straight up.

Her posture will also be forward. Your cat probably greets you with her ears erect, and this is a friendly greeting.

Ears can also signal aggression. If your cat's ears move from forward to backward, her sense of aggression has been activated. Ears moving from upright to horizontal usually indicate submissiveness, annoyance or fear.

If your cat's ears are often horizontal, she may have ear mites or an ear infection, so have that checked out by your veterinarian.

When your cat's ears are flattened against her head, it doesn't take a body language expert to see that she is probably frightened and may move to attack. Her ears are held this way instinctively when she fights, to protect them from teeth and claws.

If you are unfamiliar with a cat, ears laid back means that you should not try to touch her or pick her up. This could lead to being scratched or bitten.

The Body of the Cat

Your cat's body tells you a lot about how she is feeling. If her back is arched, she is probably angry or frightened. If it is only arched a bit, and there is no hair standing up, she may be welcoming your friendly touch.

If your cat lies on her back while purring or languishing in the sun, this indicates that she is quite relaxed. If she is lying on her back but is also growling, it could mean that she is very upset and getting ready to strike.

If your cat rubs her chin against you, she is marking her territory, in a more pleasant way than you may have heard of this being done. She does this with doorways and toys that are hers, too.

Head Position

The position of your cat's head tells you several things. When she stretches her head forward, she is trying to see a human or feline facial expression, or trying to encourage touch. It is normally a friendly position.

When your cat is in conflict, she may raise her head if she is confident or assertive, but aggressiveness usually results in a lowering of the head. A submissive or inferior cat may also lower her head. However, inferior cats that are in defensive mode may raise their heads.

If your cat has her head down and turns her head to the side to avoid eye contact, this is usually indicative of a lack of interest. Your cat also perceives something non-threatening if she uses this posture. When she is relaxed, she may pull her chin in.

Kneading of Paws

Kneading is sometimes known as "making biscuits". It's easy to see where it got this name. When your cat kneads her claws, on you or the bed, for instance, it is held over from her life as a kitten.

This is how nursing kittens massage their mother's teats to start the flow of milk. Usually, a cat is contented and happy when she kneads her claws.

The Playful Cat

When your cat is feeling playful, she has her pupils dilated a bit, her whiskers and ears forward and her tail up. Playing for a cat is a use of her hunting prowess. She may stalk a toy or you, in play, and crouch with her back end slightly higher than usual. Her butt may wiggle a little, and then she will pounce. Then your cat will grasp her toy and bite it a little, wrestle with it on the floor, and kick out at it with her back feet. This means she just killed her toy. She may play with your proffered hand in the same way.

Flehman Response

When your cat is smelling something, she may lift her head, open her mouth a bit, curl her lips back and squint her eyes. This helps her to gather additional information about the object or person she is sniffing. The sense of smell is essential for your cat. She actually has an extra organ in her olfactory system that is shared with that of the horse. It is known as the Jacobson's organ. It is found on the roof of her mouth, behind her front teeth. It is fully connected to the nasal cavity.

If your cat smells something that interests her, she will open her mouth and inhale. This sends scent molecules over this olfactory organ. It intensifies the odor and gives her more information about the object or person.

Socialization

What Is Feline Socialization?

Feline socialization normally takes place during the earliest weeks of a kitten's life. In this process, she will learn to interact properly with cats, other animals and people. She will have many experiences with the world around her, so she will become accustomed to the sounds, sights and smells that she will encounter into adulthood.

Like many young animals, kittens accomplish socialization easily, until they have reached a certain age. When they have reached the end of this period, they become more naturally wired to be suspicious of new things. This is an important part of a cat's life. The fearless and open nature of young kittens allows them to become more comfortable with things and people that they will encounter every day in their adult life.

The suspiciousness beginning after the end of socialization ensures that he will be cautious with new things. New animals or things in his environment may be dangerous, and after she has learned about socialization, she learns that she must also be wary of some things in her world.

If you have a kitten that is still young, it's important to utilize the period of socialization to introduce her to new things. This will allow her to become more comfortable as a companion animal that lives in a world of humans. This world includes many things and many people, including sights, smells, noises and sensations.

When should you socialize your kitten? She will be most respective to your socialization studies when she is between the weeks of two and seven. As long as she is handled a lot and enjoys pleasing inter-actions with people and other animals, she will likely remain a cat who is friendly to other animals and humans as she grows. In addition, new experiences will stress her less if she is socialized during the proper time.

If your kitten does not have social contact with other animal and people before she is eight or nine weeks old, she may be fearful of people and new animals for her whole life. Likewise, if you try to tame an unsocialized, feral adult cat, it will be similar to working with any wild animal. Feral cats can become more tolerant of you if they see you a lot, but they won't be social animals like socialized domestic cats.

Early handling and exposure to the environment is beneficial for kittens, but you should not separate them from their mother while they are young. Mother cats pass on social skills to their kittens, and if you wean your kittens at too young an age, they may have difficulty in relating to other animals.

If your kittens and their mother cat have a good home, simply handle them to give them that human interaction, without removing them from Mama's care. If you are adopting a kitten from a litter which hasn't had any proper socialization, six or seven weeks of age is an optimal time. This will give you a chance to expose your kitten to many new things, and allow her to become used to people.

How Do You Properly Socialize Your Kitten?

If you have the mother cat along with her litter, you need to help her to socialize the kittens. Get started at an early age, so that the kittens will become comfortable with people. Careful socializing of kittens will help them to mature into well-adjusted, wonderful pets. The more contact with humans that kittens get before they are seven week old, the friendlier they are likely to be as they grow up. Kittens who are stroked and held even for just several minutes a day will begin exploring their world sooner and be less wary of strangers and unusual events later in their lives.

If Mama Kitty is all right with you being around her litter, you can even handle newborn kittens daily. Pick them up gently, stroke them softy and place them back in the nest. Handling sessions should be short. You don't want to over-stimulate the kittens or make them uncomfortable with people. If your Mama Kitty is over-protective of her littler, perhaps you can handle the kittens for just a few minutes while the mother leaves for meals or litter box stops.

Once your kittens are full alert, with ears and eyes open and working well, and they can regulate their body temperature, they can start to meet new people and experience new things. This usually happens between three and four weeks. Handle them daily, and expose them to new sensations, smells, sounds and sights.

When your kittens are on solid food, their mother may kill prey and bring it to her family. This helps the kittens to become interested in chasing objects and pouncing on them. You can use interactive toys at this time. This is also a good time to expose your kittens to various surfaces, like grass, concrete, gravel, linoleum and carpeting.

Give Your Kittens Objects to Explore

Use paper bags, toys, packing paper and cardboard boxes for your kittens to play inside. This will allow them to learn about investigating various places with their little paws. Use different toys and bags so that they won't get bored. Scratching posts will be fun for them, too.

Exposing young kittens to new experiences is an important factor in their growth, but don't overwhelm them. Petting them gently for a few minutes a day will help in the development of their social skills. Even small input of a visual tactile and auditory nature will help them with social skills, problem solving and coordination as they mature.

Three or four weeks of age will be a good time to start the introduction of toys to your kittens. Attach toys to wands or strings so they can skitter like birds or mice. Tempting toys will exercise and entertain kittens, and teach them hunting lessons, too. Be sure to teach your kittens that human toes and fingers are not toys. Play biting is cute when kittens are young, but not as much when they are older. Redirect kittens if they want to bite you during play sessions.

Many cats only experience travel as cramped carriers and sticks with needles at the veterinary clinic. Kittens should be taken out and even taken to kitten classes to improve their socialization skills.

Kitten classes are rapidly spreading, and are a great way to introduce your kittens to other cats and other people.

Kitten socialization classes usually include just a few sessions. They may be held in the office of a veterinarian. Your kittens will need to be vaccinated first, as well as de-wormed and tested negatively for FeLV/FIV.

During these classes, your kittens will meet new people while you learn more about cat health and behavior. They also give your cat a chance for a car ride that ends in a pleasant environment.

If Your Cat Wasn't Properly Socialized While Young

If your cat or kitten was not socialized when she was young, you can still help her to function more easily in the world. It isn't impossible to help older cats become more comfortable with their surroundings. It may take longer, though.

If your cat is shy, she may become comfortable eventually with people close to you. However, fearful adult cats won't be as social. Feral cats are even more difficult to socialize, and it's wise to seek out advice from an animal behaviorist if you adopt a semi-wild cat.

Introducing a New Kitten to Your Home

In basic feline hierarchy, a new kitten will not be dominant over an adult cat you already have. Separate the existing pet and the new kitten for a couple days. Your adult cat will hear the kitten in the other room, and become more accustomed to the smell and sounds of the new kitten.

The next step is putting your new kitten in a carrier in the middle of a room, to give the two cats a chance to sniff each other. Do not be surprised if your adult cat bats at the cage, in a show of dominance. There may be hissing, too.

During the time you separate the cats, and afterwards, give them both plenty of attention. Keep them separated until they have accepted each other. Once they are comfortable loose and in the same room, lavish attention on the adult cat, too, so there won't be issues with jealousy.

Socializing Adult Cats

Adult cats are less flexible in adapting to new routines or new pets in the home. It's understandable considering that a cat, who has had all of your attention, suddenly has to share with another cat, or a dog.

Introduce your cat to the smell of the new kitten. Give her a blanket that the new kitten has slept on. Let her spend time sniffing it, so she becomes accustomed to the scent of the new kitten.

Once they know each other, feeding from separate bowls is a good idea. Keep them in the same room if you can, so that each will associate the good food with the other. After they eat and groom, they may begin grooming and bonding with the other.

Socializing Your Cat with a Dog

Introducing a new dog to your one-cat home is easier than it is to socialize two cats. Dogs enjoy company since they are pack animals. A dog will become acclimated more easily to kittens as compared to cats. Introduce the new animal smell, while keeping the dog isolated. Protect the dog when they meet, because cats are more dangerous to dogs, with their lightning-
fast claws and teeth.

Protect your cat, too. Some dogs may see smaller animals as prey. Don't leave the animals together unsupervised until they are fully socialized to each other.

How Do You Socialize a Shy Cat?

If you adopt a kitten or cat who is shy, the process may be traumatizing for your new pet. You will need to be very patient when you introduce a new cat into a home where you already have one or more cats. Work with your new cat and reassure the cat already in your home that she is still just as important to you. Socializing a shy cat can take weeks or even months, but it will be time well spent when you can all relax together.

Set Up a Space for Your New Cat

Cats are by nature territorial, but too much territory in the beginning can be a bit overwhelming for your new cat. A small room with no hiding places will work well as a temporary home. Give your new cat water, food and her own litter box in her special room. You can leave his carrier open and inside the room, with a blanket inside, for a safe spot. Soft music or music on TV may help your new cat to ease into her surroundings, too. Your new cat should remain in her safe room until she is fully socialized with your original cat. If you let her out too soon, she may find a great hiding spot, and set back your socialization efforts.

Take this step slowly. Rushing it can set your process back. You will first need your new cat to trust you. Sit with her in her room until she is comfortable coming to you. Move slowly and speak softly.

When your new cat is comfortable with you inside her room, you may try holding out your hand, with the palm facing down. Let your new cat smell you. If she approaches, hold the hand in position and speak softly to the cat. If she will allow it, stroke the top of her head. Watch her body language with care. If she backs away, you've over-stepped the boundaries with which she is comfortable right now. Don't force contact until she is ready for it.

Create Positive Experiences for Your Cat

Shy kitty can be bribed into socializing a bit by offering her tasty foods. Treats including deli meat, tuna or wet cat food may be used. Only give her these treats when you sit with her, so she associates one with the other. In this way, you'll become less fearful and a more positive experience for your shy cat.

It may take more than one session for your new cat to eat the treats in your presence. If she doesn't eat them with you in the room, take them with you when you leave the room. She needs to associate the treats with your presence.

Once your new cat is accustomed to your being in the room, she may let you begin to pet her. Proceed with patience until she lets you pet her all over. Move closer as she allows it.

When you socialize a cat who is shy, be patient. Whenever your cat is not comfortable, back up to a place where she was comfortable. Move quietly and slowly and remain calm.

Cats progress at different speeds in socialization. Some will come more quickly to you, especially if they are young. Others will take more time to learn to trust you.

Righting Reflex

Do Cats Always Land on Their Feet?

This question has been asked for centuries, eversince people noticed this uncanny ability of cats to land on their feet even when falling from heights.

Once you are up more than two or three floors, the cat is able to rotate herself in midair so that she nearly always lands on her feet. Injuries may be sustained, depending on the height from which she falls.

Cats have what is termed "nonfatal terminal velocity". This sounds like a simple contradiction, but many smaller animals have this fortuitous advantage. Once she orients herself, a cat can spread out to create an effective parachute. Some cats have fallen 20 or more stories without any injuries. As long as she doesn't land on something that could injure her, she may walk away from the fall.

The Feline Falling Study with an Inherent Flaw?

The Journal of the American Veterinary Medical Association brought out a study in 1987, in which two veterinarians examined 132 cats who fell from high windows. These cats were all brought into a New York veterinary hospital, the Animal Medical Center.

The average fall for these cats was about five and a half stories, but 90% of these cats survived, even though some had serious injuries. The veterinarians examined the data and discovered that the number of injuries like broken bones increased with the height of the fall, as one would expect. However, this was only true for the cats that fell seven stories or less. Of the cats that fell more than seven stories, the injuries actually declined. The higher the fall, above seven stories, the less chance there seemed to be of serious injury.

The authors of this study explained this result by stating that if a cat falls from more than five stories, she reaches terminal velocity – maximum downward speed – of about 60 mph. After this point, the cats were hypothesized to have spread themselves as you may have seen flying squirrels accomplish. This minimized the injuries.

It sounds logical, but there is a fatal flaw in their study, actually mentioned by posters on an unrelated online forum. The flaw? This study was only based on cats brought in for treatment. If your cat fell 20 stories and died, you wouldn't take her to a veterinary clinic. That seems to skew the results of the study, and makes high falls seem safer than they probably are.

The Animal Medical Center's Dr. Michael Garvey was not involved in the original study, but he does not feel that omitting unreported fatalities skews the statistics. He mentioned that the cats that fell from higher heights usually had injuries that suggested they had landed on their chests. This supports the theory that cats can act like flying squirrels in the air.

It was suggested that a cat landing this way had a better chance of surviving than a cat landing in a different position. Dr. Garvey feels that the study is still valid and admits that people may always disagree with any medical study.

The ability of cats to fall great distances and land on their feet is usually attributed to their "righting reflex" and to their unique skeleton structure.

The "righting reflex" is the ability of a cat to differentiate up and down, then use her natural reflexes to rotate, midair. This orients her body so that her feet will land first. This has been seen in kittens of ages as young as three weeks, and it is believed to be completely developed by the time kittens are eight weeks old.

In addition to this righting ability is a flexible backbone in the cat, and her lack of a collarbone. These factors together allow for upper body rotation and flexibility. When a cat turns her forefeet and head, the rest of her body follows and the cat can orient herself and land upright.

"High rise syndrome" is a phrase coined to describe the innate ability of cats to survive falls from great heights and land on their feet. It wasn't until scientists watched flying squirrels and cats in apparent free-fall that they noticed both have a low body ratio of volume to weight. They can slow their descent by simply spreading out. Their fluffy coats and relatively low weight allow them to use their high drag coefficient, which gives them a better chance to survive fall

In order for you to understand how a cat can land on her feet when she falls, you have to understand a few concepts related to rotational motion. A cat rotates her body as she falls.

The moment of inertia of any object – or any cat – is determined by the distance that its mass is distributed from the axis of rotation. This sounds very scientific, so it may help to picture a ball on a string that you are swinging around your head. The longer the string, the greater the moment of inertia for the ball.

Putting this back into cat terms, if a cat stretches her tail and legs, she can increase her moment of inertia. She can also decrease this moment of inertia if she curls up. The cat can manipulate her moment of inertia by extending and retracting her legs and rotating her tail. This changes the speed of her rotation, giving her control over which body part will contact the ground first.

Cats also conserve their angular momentum. When they fall, they change their orientation by reducing their rotational inertia to increase their angular speed. Stretching out their legs increases their rotational inertia and slows their speed. This gives cats the time they need to rotate their bodies so that they will land on their feet.

Cats need at least three feet of falling distance in order to have the time to right themselves before they land. Cats without tails have the same ability, using their hind legs and conserving momentum to prepare for a landing. The tail is not necessary for this righting reflex to be used.

After a cat determines up as opposed to down with her vestibular apparatus, or through visual means, she can twist herself to face down without changing her net momentum. The steps to rotate and safely land have actually been spelled out through observation:

The cat bends in the middle so the front half of her body rotates on an axis different from the rear of her body.

She tucks in her front legs to reduce the inertia moment from the front of her body and extends her rear legs to increase the rear moment of inertia. In this way, she can rotate her front half as much as 90 degrees while her rear half is rotated a lot less – as low as 10 degrees – in the opposite direction.

The cat tucks her rear legs and extends her front legs so that she can rotate her rear body a greater amount than the front of her body.

Depending on her initial angular momentum and flexibility, the cat may repeat the rotations until she has rotated a full 180 degrees.

Cats have other features that reduce possible fall damage, in addition to their righting reflex. They are small in size and have a light bone structure. Their fur also decreases the velocity of their falls. Once righted, cats may also spread their body to slow the rate of their descent.

As cats reach their terminal velocity of 60 miles per hour (as compared to 130 miles per hour for the average person), they are able to relax, which helps to prevent severe injuries on impact. Some people believe that cats orient their limbs in a horizontal level, so that their body hits the ground before their legs.

Scent Spraying and Rubbing

You probably love it when your cat comes up and rubs or strokes herself against you with her little chin. Did you know this is part of feline communication?

Scent Glands in Cats

Cats have glands in their lips, forehead, front paws and rear and flank. They secrete pheromones, which act to help your cat to communicate via chemicals. Cats produce different types of pheromones, which are capable of sending various signals. They also affect your cat's behavior.

Pheromones help your female cat let males know her reproductive status, and they tell them how receptive she will be to them. Pheromones also mark territory and objects, and you. They signal familiarity and comfort. Pheromones in cats are unique – in fact, they are as unique as human fingerprints. Cats deposit them as calling cards, to let everyone know where they have been.

Pheromones that are secreted by the facial glands usually calm your cat. When she rubs her face on objects, she leaves her scent, which is not offensive to people and which is reassuring for your cat. If another cat passes the objects, he or she may stop and smell the scent. If you have a multi-cat household, other cats may be marking the same objects.

Pheromones tell cats who has been in a certain area and when she was there. When you stroke your cat, or when she rubs against your legs, she leaves her benign scent on you, identifying you as her own.

Communicating with Scent

Cats use contact with you or objects in your home to communicate gentle reminders, or urgent needs. Your cat may just be asking for a rub, too. If you have two or more cats, you will probably see that they occasionally rub faces with each other. This is only done if the cats are comfortable in each other's presence.

The act of head rubbing between cats will create a comingling of shared scents that are helpful to cats, since they aid them in feeling more comfortable. They will also mark objects in your home to make themselves more secure in this territory.

Bumping heads is meant to be affectionate. It is something that shows that cats are not always as aloof and independent as we believe them to be. Your cat rubs against you to include you as part of her territory.

Marking Behavior

Communicating by scent is sometimes called "marking behavior". Just as cats use body language, scent is one of their primary methods of communicating with other cats. Using their scents, cats will be able to discern, even from a distance, if a cat now entering their territory is familiar or not. They also mark to leave messages for any other cats in the area. Outside of urine marking, which is much-dreaded, cats use their scent glands in a more benign way, leaving notice of their presence. Their sense of smell is keen, and some people feel that it may even rival that of dogs. Cats are not trained to search for drugs or bombs, because, unlike dogs, cats will hit on whatever interests them at the time.

Jacobson's Organ

Cats possess a special organ found in the roof of the mouth. It is known as the Jacobson's organ. Cats use it to analyze the chemicals in scents. This specialized organ is useful for any interesting smells, but it is most often used to analyze pheromones.

Bumping heads is meant to be affectionate. It is something that When your cat finds a smell that interests her, she will breathe it in through her mouth. Then it will be "tasted" in the Jacobson's organ. If your cat is using this scent organ, you can tell by looking at her.

Her mouth will be open and her lips will curl back a bit. This is known as a Flehman response. Male horses have the same type of response to mares in heat. Once you see this act once, you will recognize it when you see it again.

Urine Marking

Urine marking is also called spraying, and this is the best-known way utilized by cats to communicate by smell. It is effective for cats, useful in marking territory, exchanging information, announcing their arrival, or threatening another cat. They can disagree with each other without ever coming into physical confrontation.

Urine spraying is usually associated with male cats, but females may also spray. Neutering or spaying your cat before he or she reaches sexual maturity will generally stop the spraying behavior even before it starts. It isn't a guarantee, though. Neutered or spayed cats may spray for different reasons than mating. Urine marking is used for conveying other messages, too. Cats who are anxious or stressed may spray.

Urine marking is a natural thing for a cat to do. They don't do it out of anger or spite, and they don't know they are being "bad" when they do it. If you punish your cat for spraying, he or she may become upset and actually spray more often. Modification of the behavior is the proper way to handle urine marking.

Rubbing Is a Communication Tool

You probably hate cat spraying, but you feel very differently when your cat rubs you. Rubbing is part of social communication for your cat. Glands in the face, paw pads and tail release a scent that is unique for each cat. This communicates territory and gives visiting cats information about your cat.

When cats rub against each other as they pass, or rub on your leg, these are behaviors that are social for the cats. Rubbing signals respect and the wish to bond. Rubbing among familiar cats creates a group scent, which increases the familiarity and bonding between all the cats. This is also seen in colonies of feral cats.

Group scent production is believed to have something to do with survival instinct. When a group of cats has a group scent, they know immediately if a cat entering their area is one of their own band or not.

When your cat rubs on you, she is including you in her group, and she also adds your scent to the group of cats in your home, if you have more than one cat.

What Is Bunting?

Bunting is a bonding ritual and part of the rubbing techniques that cats use. When your cat bumps her head lightly or rubs it against another cat, or you, it is a bonding behavior. If your cat jumps into your lap, she may bunt against your hand a few times before she settles down to be petted. When you pet your cat, you are using the human rubbing version. It combines your scent with hers. Allowing your cat to rub you, and petting her, are important aspects of social bonding, and you should look forward to them.

New Cats and Rubbing

With a newer cat, especially if she is an adult, begin your bonding process by simple rubbing. Pet your cat's face and head, as long as she will allow it. You can move gradually onto her flank and then her tail, as she allows it. When cats who know each other approach in non-hostile situations, they generally greet each other by sniffing nose to nose. Then they progress to rubbing heads or bunting, and sometimes they even lick the other cat's face and ears. As a rule, the more dominant cat will initiate the rubbing.

Dominance among two or more cats does not necessarily mean aggression. Your dominant cat may be quite even-tempered, but he still occupies the top spot in the pecking order. The submissive cat or cats will wait for the dominant cat to begin sniffing or rubbing. If two cats who are not friends encounter each other, there will usually only be a bit of nose to nose sniffing.

When you greet a cat that is not familiar to you, begin by using scent communication. Extend a finger for this cat to sniff. This is a human adaptation of the cat's natural greeting of nose to nose. Don't attempt to pet a cat you don't know. After she sniffs you, if she rubs her mouth or head along your extended finger, she is letting you know that she is comfortable enough and that you may pet her.

If, on the other hand, this new cat backs up and just stares at you, consider this a challenge. Don't try to pet her, or you may be scratched or bitten.

Cat Scratching

In addition to keeping their claws in proper condition, scratching is also a way of communicating through scent, for a cat. The scent glands within the paws leave her unique sent on anything she scratches. She will usually scratch to mark territory. It leaves visual reminders (scratch marks) in addition to scent.

Scratching is a natural thing for cats to do, and shouldn't be considered as "bad behavior". Your cat doesn't try to tear up a couch because she is misbehaving or mad. She is doing it to leave her scent and impression.

If you don't want your cat scratching your favorite couch or chair, give her other things to scratch. Scratching posts work very well for most cats.

Select a type that won't fall over. Some cats like posts with sisal rope, and others prefer carpeted posts. If you have more than one cat, set up several different areas with cat trees and posts that can be scratched. The idea here is to give your cat another place to scratch, not to stop her from scratching. It is natural and normal for cats to scratch, and punishing your cat for this will only result in her becoming frustrated or afraid of you.

The Sense of Smell in Cats

Cats have a powerful sense of smell. A cat can easily identify catnip odor, even though its concentration is only one part per billion! When kittens are born, although they are blind and deaf, they can already smell things. Within a day, they will know their home from another nest or house. Each may have her own favorite nipple, too.

Smell is important for cats, since it helps them to recognize friends, enemies and others. If you have multiple cats and take one to the vet, the others may hiss when the vetted cat returns, because of all the new smells on her.

If your indoor cat gets outside, or if you move to a new home with an outside cat, she may become lost if she is more than ten feet from a smell that she knows. She needs to scent her areas, or she won't know how to get home.

If your cat was not socialized when she was a kitten, she may react poorly to changes in her environment, or intrusions of unfamiliar animals, people or objects. Even a new chair may be seen as an invader. Your cat may hide from this interloper.
Alternatively, she may rub immediately against it, so that her scent is left there.

Urine Marking and Territory
Once your cat has urinated to mark your home, you must get rid of every bit of the smell. Even if you can no longer smell it after cleaning, your cat might still smell it. A cat's sense of smell is much more powerful than yours. If you move into a house with a strong odor left by a previous cat occupant, your cat will make sure to mark over these areas.

Spend a lot of time socializing your cat when he is still young, and the marking may be less of an issue. Your cat will notice the difference in smell when you board him, take him to his groomer or vet, or even when you bring home a friend who has never been to your house before.

When you move, the transition will be less stressful for your cat if you set up just one room in your new home so that it can be her refuge. Take along something from your old house so that something will be familiar to your cat.

Take her to her special room first and let her become acclimated. This works even better for males, since they are much more likely to spray.

If the previous occupants of your new house had a cat, be sure to have the drapes, carpets and any furniture left behind shampooed thoroughly before you bring in your cat.

Body Posture

Cats are not the type of creatures that live in packs, like dogs. Their groupings are looser and not as strictly hierarchical. They will mix with others when they mate, raise kittens or live in groups like multi-cat households or hierarchical. They will mix with others when they mate, raise kittens or live in groups like multi-cat households or feral colonies.

The posture of cats and its use in body language is subtle and complex, using more than 25 visual signals in 16 unique combinations. There are more nuances that are so subtle that humans don't notice them. However, as a cat person, you may learn to recognize some of the body posturing of your cat.

Body posture is most dramatic when rivals are meeting, when territory is in question or during courtship. As a rule, cats will let others pass through their area, but the main area may be protected quite fiercely. Altered cats usually have interactions that are less extreme. Some visual signals may be displayed when cats play, with humans or other cats.

Feline body language, including its many postures, is meant to convey messages and to end or avoid physical confrontation. Both cats want to win their cases without using claws and teeth, since this could injure them both. Cat disputes are often resolved by stare-downs and yelling, rather than by violence.

Using subtle body posture, cats may resolve conflicts without humans even knowing that a showdown was in progress. The dominant cat, when he wins a confrontation, walks away from the cat who lost, and sits down. He may groom himself, too.

Look at the Whole Body

Body posture can't be read unless you look at the whole cat body. This includes not only posture, but also the face and the tail position. Looking at just one element may mislead you, since cats combine posture and movements into one message.

When a cat arches her back, she is usually upset. However, the same position in a relaxed cat may mean she would like to be rubbed.

Defensive Posture

A cat who feels defensive will erect her fur, so that she appears larger than she is. Dominant cats also attempt the "bigger" look, even accompanied by feline swaggering at times. When cats fluff up like this, they are bluffing, which is used to avoid many types of conflict.

Aggressive cats may straighten their legs, making their hind ends higher. The hair along their tail and spine will be erected into a sharp ridge. Defensive cats erect fur ridges, but also puff themselves out. They will arch their backs and position themselves facing sideways to an aggressive cat. This is another aspect of posture used to make them appear larger than they are.

If the aggressive cat pauses, defensive cats may move like crabs in a sideways direction. You may have seen kittens doing this in mock fights. This is actually a slow retreat used to avoid provoking sudden attacks.

They may even sink onto one side, to demonstrate that they are sub-missive. If the aggressor still threatens submissive cats, they may roll onto their backs, to appease the dominant cat. Dogs on their bellies are submissive, but cats can still attack from this position.

If a submissive cat is in this position and the aggressor jumps on her, she can clasp the aggressor with her forelegs, and the hind legs can scratch at the aggressor. You may have seen this type of behavior when your cat is playing with a toy.

Head Position and Posturing

The position of your cat's head in her overall posture can tell you several things. If she has her head stretched forward, she is trying to see your expression or that of another cat. She may also be encour-aging you to interact with her.

If your cat is in conflict, her posture will show a higher head if she is the dominant of the two cats, and the other cat will have her head lowered. When your cat is relaxed, she will usually pull her chin down a bit. Your cat may use her whole body to rub you or a feline friend. The posture here is relaxed and friendly.

Humans are very much creatures of eye contact. Your cat does not usually prolong eye contact unless it is to convey assertiveness or when she is threatening another animal. In a room full of people, your cat perceives those looking at her as threatening, which is why she will almost always walk over to someone who is ignoring her.

Cats who are rivals may use staring to resolve a conflict. If your cat realizes someone is looking at her, she may assess what she perceives to be a threat, before going on with her previous activity. She may be self-conscious, though. She will become uncomfortable if she is watched studiously.

If you want to reassure your cat after you've been watching her, you can blink slowly. This breaks up your "aggressive" stare and reassures her that you don't mean anything with the stare. Yawning is reassuring, too.

Your cat has excellent peripheral vision and doesn't often stare right at something, unless she is getting ready to pounce on a moving object. When your cat daydreams, she does not appear to be looking at anything. However, she is taking in information with her peripheral vision.

The Feline Mouth

Cats do not often use their mouths as a signal of aggression. When your cat opens her mouth to yawn, this is usually interpreted as a non-threat. Open-mouthed hisses or snarls show a cat that is defensive and frightened. Growls are usually done with just a slight opening of the mouth.

Sometimes, cats look like they are angry when they are not. If your cat has her ears back and her eyes are narrow slits, it may appear like anger, but she could actually be yawning. Ears may be partly flattened when cats yawn widely.

Cats may sit with their tongues sticking out just a bit. This usually shows relaxation and a sense of contentment. It can be a comical look, but they are usually concentrating. If your cat licks her lips, it may indicate anticipation or anxiety, depending on her surroundings. The fullest use of lip licking is done when cats clean themselves after they eat.

Body Posture and Whiskers

Whiskers are used for judging closed-in areas or object proximity, but this is not their only purpose. They also are indicative of your cat's mood. When your cat is relaxed, her whiskers are relaxed, too, and held slightly off to the side of her head.

If she is interested in something, her whiskers may perk forward. The pads of her cheeks may appear to swell as these muscles pull her whiskers into the position she wants.

If your cat is afraid, she may pull her whiskers back alongside her cheeks, in a non-threatening posture.

Feline Ears

The ears of a cat are very mobile. There are 20-30 muscles that control them, so they can move easily up and down and through a 180-degree arc. Sometimes they are flattened backwards or sideways, and sometimes they are pricked forward.

Cats can move their ears independently, whether panning around like radar dishes or scanning for nearby sounds. When added to posture, they can communicate effectively.

When your cat is relaxed and contented, her ears usually face forward but may tilt back a bit. Even when she is half-asleep, her ears will tell you that she is still alert.

When your cat senses a movement or noise, she will prick her ears and sometimes swivel one or both ears to track the noise source.

If your cat becomes anxious, her ears will move back slightly and flatten. Fearful cats have lowered ears. When a cat is fearful but still aggressive, her ears will flatten down sideways.

Ears may be used for flagging or flicking, when the ear is moved horizontally as it is flattened. This may be a way cats use to point. Your cat may be deciding between two things, like going to her chair or going outside, when her ears are flagging.

It's All about the Tail

Your cat's tail helps her to balance, and present a confident posture. It also helps her to maneuver at higher speeds. The tail is also a way cats use to communicate. If your cat is hunting – play or for-real – her tail will be almost horizontal behind her. This keeps it from becoming entangled in shrubs.

A twitching tail means that your cat is concentrating and interested in something. This is often the case when your cat is at the window and sees a bird or a squirrel outside.

Your cat's tail helps her in communication with you and with other cats. It is quite mobile, with the ability to move up or down and side to side. It may move slowly or thrash like a whip. A curled tail during sleep means your car is very relaxed.

A cat who is urine marking will have his tail up and quivering as he treads and dances with his hind feet, in an effort to raise his rear end higher. When your cat greets you, she may extend her tail and quiver it, but this is not related to spraying. It is her way of saying she is very happy to see you.

When young cats greet their mother, they will run to her with up-right tails. They rub or droop their tails around their rumps to solicit a feeding. Adult cats twine their tails, too. They rub against other cats who are friends and twine their tails together.

Most people recognize the so-called bottle brush tail. When a cat has a defensive posture and is threatened, the tail can double in size, as her spinal hair stands erect. It makes her look bigger so that her aggressor will leave her alone.

Posture and Hugging

If you have ever hugged your cat tightly, you may have learned that she doesn't like it. Cats do not like being confined. They prefer simple stroking. Some cats do like hugs, but they are in the minority. If your cat wriggles away when you try to hug her, she is saying, "Thanks, but no thanks.

Cats use their posture to establish or smooth over relationships. If your cat wanders into another cat's territory, she will apologize and use postures to avoid a fight.

A confident cat will face unknown things head-on. While using this posture, your cat can defend herself or strike, if necessary. A cat that is fearful turns sideways and arches her back, to get away from the perceived threat.

Cats who are surrendering to another cat flatten themselves low to the ground, to appear small. They will tuck in all four feet and hold their tail and ears tightly against their bodies.

Cats who are feeling affectionate may groom you or another cat. They may ask you to play by rolling over and presenting you their tummies. They can also play with you, or cuddle and sleep with you. If your cat sleeps with her back to you, she is showing you the ultimate trust.

Bumping hips and touching noses are signs of affection and trust between cats. If your cat jumps onto your lap and presents you with her backside, this is her equivalent of a handshake. She doesn't mean to offend you by showing you her rear end.

Kneading

When your cat kneads, she rhythmically alternates her paws, pushing against soft objects or your lap. Some cats don't use their claws when they knead, while others do. Some cats even knead with all four paws. There are cats that do not knead, but it is very common for young and old cats.

Why do cats knead? There are various ideas about this topic, as there are about many aspects of cat behavior. Some cats purr and knead when you pet them, but they might also do it while sitting alone on your bed, for no apparent reason. Cats start kneading when they are young. When kittens nurse, they knead to stimulate the flow of milk in their mother's nipples. However, no one knows exactly why they carry this habit beyond the nursing age.

Your Cat May Knead You

Your cat may enjoy kneading in your lap while she is being petted. Unfortunately, if she uses her claws in this action, it can be painful for you. You may try to pet her on the belly instead, but not all cats are fond of that. You will not want to punish your cat if she hurts you while she is kneading. She does not realize that you are hurting. If you use nail guards or keep her nails trimmed, it can be easier on you when she kneads.

Stretching

Cats have their own type of yoga, and it works out their muscle kinks just as stretching does for you. Kneading is a way cats can keep their muscles limber. Your cat's feral ancestors preferred sleeping on soft surfaces. They would often knead leaves or tall grasses to make a bed – or a nest, if a mother lion or tiger was having cubs. Kneading also allows cats to be sure there are not unwelcome rodents lying in the foliage.

Kneading for Territorial Reasons

Cats are very territorial, and kneading with their paws leaves their scent on their belongings. This includes you, too. Cats activate the scent glands in the pads of their paws to mark things or people by kneading. Female cats sometimes knead their paws before they go into heat. This is a display for male cats that they are available and ready to mate.

Kneading Is Instinctive

Kneading is instinctive, even after a cat is no longer nursing from her mother. Adult cats who knead may be doing it to:
- Calm themselves when stressed
- Show contentment
- Mark their human with their scent
- Mark objects with their scent

One old theory said that adult cats who kneaded were taken away from their mothers at too early an age. This was debunked long ago, since almost all cats knead. It seems to be quite simply something that comforts them, whether they are happy or stressed.

Kneading may become obsessive for some adult cats. They may even suckle on clothing, blankets or stuffed toys while they knead.

Feline Intelligence

Dog and cat owners enjoy bragging about the intelligence level of their favorite pets. There is a long debate about whether cats are smarter than dogs. Not surprisingly, the owners of each type ofpet feel that their pet is smarter.

The Dog versus Cat Intelligence Debate

Dog owners point to the fact that their pets can perform tricks. Cat owners feel that their pets are simply too intelligent to perform tricks on command. The question isn't as easy as that, though – it's the animal equivalent of comparing apples and oranges.

Dogs are primarily pack animals, and they need to follow their top dog, which in domestic settings is their owner. Cats are more solitary and do not answer to anyone. Their only motivation is survival. While cats don't often perform tricks, they are certainly adaptable and clever, in their own way.

Cats are self-reliant and resourceful, and have lived for thousands of years in many diverse environments. Even your domestic cat shows a versatile, strong-willed and crafty nature.

Mastering Cat Language

Your cat's remarkable physical and mental abilities are often thought of as simply instinctive. However, they take time to master their language and hone the abilities with which they are born. Cats do not learn in the same way as dogs. They have their own unique type of intelligence.

Cats Don't Forget

Once your cat attains knowledge, whether through trial and error or accident, that knowledge will be retained for her whole life. She has an excellent memory. Techniques in hunting, even while largely unused, can be easily recalled if your cat ever wanders off and has to fend for herself.

Cats are easily frightened, so they retain strong memories of incidents that they consider threatening. They also store and recall happy experiences, especially those related to play or food.

Domestic cats respond very well to sounds that are familiar to them, like the opening of a can of cat food. Many cats also know when it's mealtime, even if there is no other way to know in addition to hungerand an internal clock of some sort.

Tricks and Training

As the psyche of cats has become more understood, felines have been trained for performance in films and TV series. They don't perform for a pat on the head, but they can be trained with food. Cats learn especially well if their owner is the trainer and if play or food is involved as a reward.

 The owners of cats claim that their pets are simply too smart to do the types of tricks that you have seen dogs do. Other people are naysayers when it comes to the subject of feline intelligence, since they won't do tricks as easily as dogs will.

Testing animal intelligence is not always humane. Researchers used to insert electrodes into a cat's brain to stimulate behaviors or to monitor the cat's brain activity. Subjects have been killed by inhumane testing.

More recently, tests have been performed in settings more natural for domestic cats. Tests should take into account the innate behavior of animals, as well as their instincts.

In tests where dogs and cats were navigating mazes, cats did not perform well, as far as humans were concerned. Dogs learned their way through the maze to reach a reward. Cats relaxed and looked into blind alleys and took baths. Cats are not as motivated to seek treats as dogs are. The blind alley investigations made sense for cats, because who knew what prey there might be inside them?

Dogs are more likely to cooperate in tests that show how eager they are to please their masters. Dogs have also been bred over the years to reduce some traits and to enhance ease of training. Cats have different social structures. Male cats often wander, looking for females, rather than remaining in a group. When large food sources are found, they may form loose colonies. However, the social structure is closer to that of a pride of lions than to a pack of dogs.

Cooperating with humans, for cats, is only limited, unless the cats' interests are served when they perform tasks. Dogs have been bred for many years to make them more useful for people. Cats are mainly bred for appearance. This doesn't mean that they are less intelligent; it simply means that they don't need to do tricks to get what they need.

Response to Stimuli

Early psychologists felt that all types of behavior were the result of stimulus and response. Their first theories did not leave room for innate behaviors, instinct, consciousness, thinking or predispositions to specific behaviors. Learning, when reduced to its simplest level, means associating stimuli that were previously unrelated. Learning also involves the assessment of actions and their consequences.

Present experiments are geared to provide a more complete knowledge of the psychology of felines. Electrodes placed in the brains of cats don't always tell scientists what they need to know, other than the fact that cats mainly react to hunger, thirst and other vital stimuli.

Psychologists in the past believed that all learning was simply association. The response to stimuli was even considered to be true in the case of humans, too. Today, it is understood that many breeds of mammals have mental processes that are more complex.

Many higher animals have their own representation of the world they live in, and how it works. They consult this world when they make decisions. It will never be completely possible to understand the way cats perceive or understand their world. Virtual reality gives us some idea of how the world sounds and looks like for cats. In order to fully investigate the intelligence of felines, and their ability to learn, more humane testing is needed, and this testing must be better suited for cats. In order for this to happen, researchers need to know how today's cats have evolved in a way that suits their lifestyle and environment. There will always be some things that predispose cats to behave in specific ways.

Cats in Their Natural Environment

In the natural environment of a cat, an unconditioned stimulus may be something as simple as pain that was inflicted by a tomcat. The response to this unconditioned stimulus may involve flight, in order to avoid further pain.

After one experience, the sight of an aggressive tomcat (which is now considered conditioned stimulus) may cause flight. This is a conditioned response, since the cat's motivation is avoiding pain. Conditioned learning can be more complicated, when you consider your cat's innate behaviors. Her ears hone in on noises, so experiments may utilize sounds, followed by food. However, testing isn't that easy. Actual research has shown that, instead of running for the food, cats searched the area of the loudspeaker over which the sound was broadcast. This does not mean that cats are dumb. To the cats, the sound indicated prey, so they went directly to the source of the sound.

What Is Intelligence?

Humans bias their studies by assessing other species' intelligence by relating it to our own. Animals with dexterous hands and good eyesight are rated highly. However, cats cannot react to stimuli by using their "hands". Cats are not less intelligent because they do not respond like monkeys in certain tests. They may be less cooperative, but that doesn't make them dumb. Animals like cats that rely on instinct can readapt only at a pace that is determined by mechanisms in their evolution. Cats can actually solve problems outside their adaptations to their niche in the environment. These abilities allow cats to cope with unexpected changes, but they are difficult to measure.

A domestic cat, left to her own devices, will take on some of the behaviors of feral cats, once she realizes that she is on her own. Her kittens may be born feral, but if they are adopted back into the human world, they will revert to the behavior of domestic cats, as long as they are socialized when they are very young.

IQ and Cats

Humans quite often define animal intelligence in the terms of "IQ". There are various scoring systems used in IQ tests, and you can learn how to perform them better. Some very intelligent people don't do well on standard IQ tests because those tests are biased to logical reasoning, or are skewed, culturally.

Cats and dogs don't need to understand the same things you do, in order to survive. The intelligence of animals is linked to their natural environment and their basic survival needs. Humans must adapt their perception of what intelligence is, and formulate tests that are appropriate for the animals they are studying.

Different types of animals have very different innate behaviors. If let loose into a group of baby ducks, a dog may try to herd them, while a cat may try to attack them, in search of food. This doesn't mean that either animal is less intelligent. Each animal performed based on his or her innate instincts.

CONLUSION

I hope this book has proven useful to you and given you a better understanding of how to take care of your persian cat.

In closing, remember to keep a watchful eye on your persian's health and never be afraid to seek your vet's advice, no matter how trivial a problem may seem.

If you do that, you can look forward to many more happy years together!

For more information on the persian cat please visit
http://ilovemypersian.co

Made in United States
North Haven, CT
22 November 2022

27091299R00062